"And the end of all our exploring
will be to arrive where we started
and know the place for the first time"
T.S. Eliot

Typeset by: Simon Heighway
Cover Image by: Allan Heighway
Author Image by: Mandy Zammit
Cover Design by: Andreas Varnavides
Art Direction by: Tree Produce

ISBN: 9781983317170

Dedication

I would like to dedicate this to everyone who has been a part of my life story... including those I've yet to meet.
I'd also like to make a little mention of some very special people:
My Mum and Dad, for their unconditional love. Always.
My Sister Mandy, for being my best friend and partner-in-crime.
My little Nephew Jim, for changing life more than anyone else. In the most beautiful ways imaginable.
My Nanna and Grandpa, for always being there for me. I know you still are..
To my dear friend Anthony, I could never have done it without you.
To my oldest friends Daz and Kev, for being there throughout it all.
To Andreas, without your Art this Earth is just 'eh'
And to Sandy, for giving me the gift of life itself..
There have also been so many people who have inspired and supported me from near and far...
But the following few deserve a very special mention...
Nicole, Valerie, Jon K, Myla, Chez, Coralie, Paola, Shorty, Jamie C, Vic, Lisa, Joseph, Lenita

And last, but by no means least, I've gotta say a great big thank you to God, or 'The Universe', for bringing all of these wonderful people into this life experience in the first place.

Time After Time

Reflections from a spiritual journey home

Contents

'Introduction'

What follows are a selection of short stories, mainly
from my own life. I've also rewritten and included a
few more famous stories and anecdotes that I've heard
throughout the years. Each one has made a deep and
lasting impression on me in its own way..

Someone once said that the Universe is not made of
atoms, but of tiny stories. I love that and I think it's so
true.
Each of our lives is a story composed of countless other
stories and, of course, each of our life stories overlap
with one another..
My life is nothing out of the ordinary, but it has had
some extraordinary moments. In fact, I believe if you
look carefully you will see that everyone's life is full
of these moments. Little moments of magic, of love, of
laughter. Those moments when you look back and see
how everything fits together, or perhaps just look up
and thank the mysterious power of the universe for
another miracle..
My own life has been slightly different in some ways,
as you'll see. But I've always tried to stay true to myself
even if that's meant breaking all the rules..
With that in mind, please note that I write in much the
same way.
I try to keep it as real, as authentic, as possible.
And I often write as I speak, even if that means
breaking many of the rules in the process.

So, I hope you find something in the following pages
that resonates. Something that you can relate to,
something you recognise from your own life too...
But more than that I hope you find a few reasons to
smile, perhaps even shed a tear...
If you come away from it all feeling good, or seeing
aspects of life through new eyes, then that's more than

a dream come true for me.
And if there's one thing I know for sure, it's that dreams
do come true..
Hope you enjoy x

There was once a child made completely of salt who very much wanted to know who he was.

He'd travelled far and wide, over mountains and through forests, searching for this truth..

But still he did not know the answer to this most basic of questions.

Until, one day, he arrived at the shore of a vast ocean..

He walked toward the edge, dipped his toe in and it disappeared.

In that moment he heard a voice.. "If you wish to know who you are, do not be afraid"

So he continued on, deeper and deeper, his body dissolving with each step..

Until eventually there was nothing left, but the ocean..

And it was in that moment he realised..

"Ahhhhh, now I know who I am"

After carving one of the most incredible statues the world had ever seen Michelangelo was asked what his secret was..

And his answer was beautiful.. "I saw the angel in the marble and just carved until I set him free"

He believed the perfect statue already existed within the rock and all he had to do was carve away everything that wasn't it.

People often ask me about my philosophy on life, and spirituality..

And this is it.

You don't have to become something you're not, or gain something you don't already have. It's more the other way around.

All you've got to do is find ways to get rid of, or strip away, all of the baggage, the conditioning, the crap, that we each accumulate over a lifetime...

To give up anything that isn't really true to who you are.

You've just gotta set that inner angel free..

And it's the art of letting go..

That's all I know.

'In My Heart'

It was a night much like any other...
I was about 6, possibly 7, years old and my Mum had just tucked me into bed...
She asked if I would like to hear a little story and, of course, I answered "Yeah, pleeease.."
I loved her little stories, but more than anything I loved the fact that they would allow me to stay up just that little bit later than usual.
She began to tell me a sweet tale of a little boy...
In all honesty, much of what she said next is still a blur...
But I do remember clearly how she told me that this little boy had grown in his 'Mummy's heart, but not her tummy'
Then she whispered.. "And that little boy was You.."

It was her beautiful way of telling me that I'd been adopted at birth.

That story was the beginning of many other stories...
And such a wonderful journey of self-discovery.

'Trust In Life'

People often ask me how, and why, I have this deep trust for whatever happens in life?

This attitude of "Fuck it", but with a twist of 'Everything happens for a reason'...

This simple knowing that there is some kind of higher, stronger, deeper power at work in our lives all the time.

Well, after decades of soul-searching and a few conversations with my nearest and dearest, I believe I finally have a coherent answer...

It is simply because my own life was saved, and I was taken care of, from the very beginning...

Perhaps even before that?

I've often heard it said that before we're born we somehow, from a place we could never imagine, choose the circumstances we are born into. That we choose our parents, our surroundings, our circumstances and the general trajectory we might take through life.

I know some people are horrified by this thought, especially those that didn't have particularly good childhoods, parents and so on..

But it kinda makes sense to me when you remember that those choices were made from a place where fear does not exist.

And from that place you see only the good that could come out of every situation. Especially the challenges.

So, in a sense I do feel that this is what happens.

Although my own story was a little different...

Because I could've ended up anywhere. Literally.

But I ended up in a family that is, to me, full of the most wonderful and special people imaginable.
And that is why I've always trusted life.

Sometimes I go out for these long and magical walks where I reflect on how lucky I got and how blessed I really am.
But the simple truth is, it could've all been so very different.
The circumstances surrounding my birth meant that I was adopted by the most amazing, kind and caring people I could ever have chosen.
Maybe, on some level, I did.
But as I've grown through this life I have heard so many stories about things that happened back then that very nearly changed everything. Yet, somehow, seemingly against all the odds, everything fell into place just as it was meant to.
And while life has been so very eventful it has also been very beautiful too. Full of love, ever since day one.
I've been a very lucky boy and not a day goes by that I don't feel so grateful.
To have actually lived this experience leaves me with the absolute faith that we are all taken care of by this Universe at all times.
Because no human being anywhere could have organised, or orchestrated, the events that needed to happen for me to end up in the family, in the life, that I eventually ended up in...
The Universe literally rearranged itself and worked its magic.

And that's why I've always believed and I always will believe that everything works out for the best.
It's the very story of my life.

So whenever people ask me how I can live in such a 'surrendered' way, just going with the flow, I tell them "If you were me, you would too". But I always remind them that it's the same for everyone.

I was just lucky enough to recognise it very early on.

I wonder if perhaps all of this is really just my way of saying a massive Thank You to my Mum and Dad for being the best parents I could ever have chosen?

Because whether I chose them, or the Universe did, no-one could've chosen better.

Perhaps it's also a little thank you to God, whatever that word really means, for taking care of me since before I even got here and ever since...

I know I've been hard work at times and I'm sorry.

But, Thank You.

Because from the very beginning you taught me the greatest lesson I could ever have learnt...

Just. Trust. Life

'New Home, Best Friends'

My parents had made the move for us, my Sister and I..
They figured that life - for a variety of reasons - may be just a little better here.
But I know they also worried that we'd find it hard to leave our friends and adjust.
London had always been home...
It's the place I was born and it's where I spent my early years.
Actually, for a very big part of my life it was all I really knew for sure of my roots..
So it would always be very close to my heart.

But in February of 1982, when I was 7 years old, my family packed up and moved to a beautiful village called Weeley in Essex...
We were now surrounded by fields and just 10 minutes from the beach.

On my first day at my new school I was introduced to my teacher, Mrs Baldwin. I didn't know it then, but she would become my favourite teacher ever and probably the best teacher I had during my whole school life.
She sat me down on a table next to two cheeky looking little rogues, Darren T and Kevin K.
They were each charged with looking after me and showing me around. I think they turned it into some kind of competition between them to see who could do the best job...
Little did I know back then that Kev and Daz would become like the brothers I never had. They would be my very best friends throughout my life.

We would remain side by side through everything.

Looking back, I'm pretty sure it was destiny which sat me in that chair that day.

When the bell rang for the end of school my Mum was waiting there, with a big smile on her face, ready to pick me up.
I told her excitedly about my 'new bestest friends' and I told her there was actually a field at the back of the school with 'real life cows' in it..
I think it was then that my parents realised they'd done the right thing..

They knew we'd be happy here.

The old man gestured towards a glass...

"You see this glass" he said.. "I love this glass. It's beautiful, it's so beautiful..

It holds the water perfectly and it glistens in the light delightfully..

I appreciate it so much.. Because it's already broken"

The glass looked fine and the boy asked the old man what he meant?

"Well, one day I will knock it by accident, or the wind will catch it, and it will fall to the floor and smash..

Eventually it will happen, I know that. It's inevitable.

So, I choose to appreciate it so much as it is..

Because one day it will be gone"

The boy understood what the old man was trying to say...

And that it was a metaphor for everything in life.

'Nanna'

It was 7th November 1986
A day that changed my life forever..

My Nanna and I were so close. I had lived with her and
my Grandpa, together with my parents, in a big house
in London during the early years of my life.
When we'd moved to Essex, Nanna and my Grandpa
had joined us a few years later and ended up living in a
beautiful house just three doors away...
So we were always extremely close, bestest pals.

Even though I didn't know the details I knew that she
had been taken into hospital the night before.
Looking back, I imagine my family didn't want me
to worry, or perhaps thought I was just too young to
understand.
But I will never forget my Mum coming to me with
tears in her eyes, sitting me down and telling me
"Your Nanna was tired Son, she really wasn't well.. and
she's had to go to Heaven"

All I remember was the shock, the sadness and the fact
that I couldn't understand where she had gone.

That was a question which I would spend much of my
life trying to answer.

'The Biggest Secret'

My school years were pretty eventful. Though mainly full of fun.

Well, at least, fun for me.. probably not for the teachers!!

Perhaps I should've taken everything a little bit more seriously. But still, I managed to learn to read and to write and I left with a smile on my face and a few decent qualifications.

However, it probably speaks volumes that out of everything I ever learned in my schooldays the following little story, that I heard when I was still quite young, was by far my favourite thing of all...

It had been a long and very busy week and God had finally finished creating everything.

It was all done. All the worlds, all the creatures, all of life...

He was happy with his work and he kicked back to relax.. But it wasn't long before he realised he'd forgotten something very important...

Where, oh where, should he put the 'Secret of all secrets'?

This was a big question and he felt he needed a little help.

So he gathered around him some of his most trusted friends and asked each one of them what they thought.

"Put it in the middle of the desert" said a Camel "They'll never find it there"

"No, no, no.. Hide it on top of the highest mountain"

said an Eagle "Only a few will ever go up there"
"Or at the bottom of the sea" said a Fish.. "It'll be almost
impossible to find..."

But God was still unsure, because he wanted to make it
well within reach for everyone to discover.

So he turned to the Wise Old Owl.. "What do you
think?" he asked the Owl.
"Hmmmm. Well, let's look at this. You want it there for
them all. Not too hidden, but not too easy to find..
Oh, I think I have it.. Yess.. Put it inside each of them.
Inside their hearts.."
God liked the idea, but asked the Owl "Why?"
"Well..", said the Owl, quite pleased with himself..
"Because it really is the last place they'll ever look!!"

'Overdosed'

My best friend Darren and I would often go on these little road trips...

Usually we'd head down to the Brighton area to deliver stuff for his work. And we'd spend the whole journey reminiscing and laughing about all the things that had happened in the 30+ years we'd known one another.

But there was a detail I told him one particular day that even he didn't know and it made me realise that not many people knew this at all...

In the early 90's I was in such a mess, I was so far off the rails...

I just thought it was great to live a rock and roll lifestyle, take every drug possible, drink way too much for anyone and get into all the trouble I could find.

My nearest, dearest, friends and family really thought I'd never make it out alive.

And I secretly thought the same.

I was just completely destructive, almost with a 'death wish', and one particular night sticks in people's minds more than most.

It was a night that everything finally caught up with me.

I was 18 years old at the time.

I had already taken almost every drug imaginable...

But, always looking for more, I had gone on to someone's house where there was an after-party.

There was a guy there, someone I didn't know, a friend of a friend, and it turned out that he was a heroin addict.

We spoke for a while and I noticed he had with him
a jar of green liquid. It was like nothing that I'd ever
seen before and I soon discovered it was a drug called
'Methadone'...

Well, me being me, I asked him if I could have some?
However, he was very reluctant to share it..

Still, a little later on, he fell asleep and I got another
friend to pour me a large cup of this stuff which I drank
almost straight away.

And it wasn't long before I realised that something was
really, really wrong...

It's hard to describe exactly how I felt, but I can tell
you that I'd never ever felt that way before.

Of all the drugs I'd experimented with over the years,
this seemed very different.

And I had a strong feeling that I should head to the
hospital...

An old friend arrived who lived near to me, so I asked
him if he would give me a lift. But I decided I would
head home rather than to the hospital.

Still, I knew I could never go into my parents house in
such a state..

So instead of going straight indoors, I headed to a
garage just along the road from my where my parents
lived.

I was taking driving lessons at the time and my 'silver
bullet' - a little old blue and silver Ford Fiesta - was
parked in there..

So I climbed into the back and I fell asleep.

Well, the next thing I knew I woke up in the hospital.

I was attached to all kinds of different machines and all
I could see around me were the terrified looks on the

faces of my Mum, my Dad and my Sister.

I had overdosed.

In fact, according to the paramedics who had arrived on the scene.. I had literally 'died' in the back of that little car.
I don't know how long I'd 'died' for and I probably never will.
But my Mum had just sensed that something was very wrong and, for some reason, she was inspired to come and look for me in my car.
A place she had never ever looked before.
And she found me there like that.
Lifeless.

She immediately called my Dad who had used all of his strength to somehow pull me out of the car before giving me the kiss of life.
They saved my life that day.
And I had known nothing about any of it.
I just woke up in that hospital where I had to spend the next few days..
Which meant that I had plenty of time to reflect...

Although it was only later on that I realised more than one miracle had actually happened that day,
And this is the detail that even my friend Darren didn't know...

I'd had a long conversation with the guy I'd got the drug from, the heroin addict, and we had planned that on the following Tuesday I would meet him and inject heroin for the very first time.
It was a plan I know I would've followed through on...
Only I couldn't, because I was still in the hospital.

I heard recently that the guy I was supposed to meet is dead now and I've no doubt that I would be too if I'd gone down that same path.

So, I really was a very lucky boy.

I had somehow dodged the bullet of all the horrendousness that comes along with heroin.

I guess the real moral of the story is that sometimes things can happen that appear to be awful at the time, but they happen for a reason...

And it's only when you look back that you see how it all fits together.

I've come to understand that God, or the Universe, or whatever you choose to call it, has a profound way of taking care of us all...

And it's always right there with us, even in the darkest of times.

In fact, especially then.

One evening a man was out hiking..

But it was getting late, cold and dark.

He had become so absorbed is his own thoughts that he'd wandered way off course and quickly realised he was completely lost.

Soon it was pitch-black and he began to feel a little afraid.

He didn't know the area very well and there were lots of cliffs and steep drops all around him.

But still, he had little choice but to continue on...

Until, suddenly, something underneath him gave way and he fell...

He tumbled down and down and just as he was about to fall over a rocky ledge he managed to grab on to a branch.

But he was now just hanging there.. In the middle of nowhere.. Holding on for dear life..

With no way to climb back up and nothing but darkness below him.

"Help! Somebody!! Please... Help me!" he cried out.

But no one came. It was such a desolate place.

He was terrified.

His hands were freezing cold and he was slowly losing his grip on the branch...

And there was no one to help!!

In sheer desperation the man, who was an atheist, called out to God,

"Please... please... if you're there... God... please help me, save me and I will believe in you always!!"

And then, to his amazement, a voice echoed all around him,
"Trust Me... Let Go... I've Got You... Trust In Me."

The man looked around him and below him and thought for a moment...
But then he mumbled to himself, "Let go? Trust? You must think I'm mad? No way!"

I think that many people find themselves in this man's situation. Perhaps not actually hanging from a branch in the dark wilderness but, never-the-less, in a desperate situation where all of their deepest instincts are telling them to just let go, to surrender. To give themselves to a higher deeper power or energy of some kind. To just drop... Into the unknown, with pure trust. But they are so full of doubt and fear that they just cling on instead.

The alternate ending to this story is that the desperate man, sensing he has little choice, decides to let go.
And he falls with faith into the void...
Then moments later he finds himself on solid ground.
It had been so dark that he just hadn't realised the ground was no more than a few feet below him.
He was safe and unharmed.
And what's more, it turns out that the ground he landed on was a pathway; the pathway he had been searching for all along - the route back home

To me, this is all just a lovely metaphor for having the courage to trust what is deepest within us and all around us.
No matter what, to have enough trust to surrender to ourselves.

Because then we will get a beautiful surprise...
We'll discover the dark void is really nothing to be
fearful of...

And the 'ground' below is actually the "Ground of
Being", which is another way of saying God, which is
just another way of saying our truest, realest Nature.
And that is most definitely the way back home.
Always

'Thank My Lucky Stars'

We'd all had a few glasses of wine and were laying in the Moroccan desert after spending the last few days trekking through the High Atlas mountains..
It was a charity thing that had sounded like a great way to have an adventure while at the same time helping a good cause.
It was an adventure that truly opened my eyes to how beautiful this world really is and how wonderful it can be to spend time in nature...
I was 22 years old.

I lay there looking up at the sky and for the first time in my life I could actually see how many millions of stars there really are.
That night I saw plenty of shooting stars too and I'm pretty sure I made some wishes which would come beautifully true in the years that followed.

It had already been an interesting, amusing evening...
One of the things about wandering in the desert wilderness was that when the time came to use the toilet you had to, er, 'burn your own waste'. Probably so that in the event of a sandstorm anyone nearby wouldn't get a face full of so much more than sand!
I had wandered off to discretely use the bathroom and done what had to be done. Then I'd wrapped everything up nice and neatly, covered it in petrol and set fire to it...
But as I wandered back to camp I heard a 'Whooosh' in the distance behind me...
I turned around and saw that I'd burned down the whole makeshift toilet block...

And the fire had lit up the desert sky for all to see...
I guess perhaps I used a bit too much fuel!!

Anyway, a couple of friends and I had decided to be
daring and sleep outside.
No tents for us that night!!
With a sleeping bag covering me and a pile of clothes
for a pillow I drifted off into a peaceful, deep sleep..
Underneath those countless beautiful shining stars.
But when the morning came I awoke to the sound of
laughter and saw a huge crowd of fellow wanderers all
looking over..

My stuff was literally everywhere.
Sleeping bag over there to my right, clothes way over
there to my left..
I wondered what on earth had happened?

It turned out that during the night everyone in the tents
had been woken by an enormous roar "It sounded like
a train" they all said.
Well, it was a train... Of camels...
As the sun came up and everyone else watched from a
safe distance, a caravan of countless camels had passed
by with my friends and I in their path.
They had walked right over us.
The wine had, no doubt, helped us sleep throughout the
whole episode.
But looking down I could see hoof prints either side of
where my head had been laying...

I don't know if we were extremely lucky that night, or
if that's just the cleverness of camels?
But I do know it won me a prize for 'Funniest moment
of the week'
And I think that place is where my deep love for being
in nature was born.

'Adrift'

It was the Summer of 1997...

I'd left a pretty good job and headed out to the Greek Islands looking for adventure.

But also.. looking for some solitude, some peace and perhaps even to 'find myself'.

I eventually got all of those things, but not quite in the way I expected...

Someone I'd worked with had told me about a beautiful quiet little village called Bali on the island of Crete.

So this is where I'd decided to go. It was perfect.

I was renting a little apartment that was kind of built into the side of a mountain.

Each day I would head out and explore.

Everyone was so friendly, even though I pretty much kept myself to myself.

It was absolute bliss.

But one day, that all changed...

I'd been offered a job in a bar which was about a mile from where I was staying...

And to celebrate I'd stayed in the bar until the very early hours.

The following morning, feeling pretty rough, but with another perfect blue sky above, I thought I'd just head to the beach and lay in the sun..

And so that's exactly what I did.

After a while I decided it may be fun to float around on the sea instead...

On a transparent lilo!

It was beautiful, just laying there, without a care in the world.

But in my hungover state I had forgotten all about sunscreen.

And it wasn't long before I drifted off to sleep...

At the same time I was drifting further and further out to sea

When I eventually woke I could barely even see land and I knew straight away that I had been badly burnt.

Somehow, by hook or by kruk, I managed to get back to the shore.

I headed straight to my apartment, but knew even then I'd been burned like never before.

As evening came I realised just how bad it really was.

By now I was in too much pain to even move.

So I just lay there...

For what seemed like an eternity.

I still don't know if it was heatstroke, sunstroke, or just severe sunburn. But my mind was all over the place...

For days.

I barely ate and I drank what little water I had.

I realised that no-one in the world actually knew where I was. None of my family, none of my friends...

I'd wanted it that way, but it didn't seem like such a great idea now.

I was in such a bad state that I honestly thought I might die...

All alone. There in my apartment. Thousands of miles from home.

It was then that I reflected back on my life...

Many people say your life flashes before your eyes when you actually die?? Well, maybe, maybe not...
But I found that the things I was looking back on were not actually the BIG things...
It was none of the big adventures, epic moments, or any of that... But instead, strangely, it was the little things.
Those intimate moments. The moments of love, magic, laughter and happiness.
I reflected on family Christmas's, the magic of Christmas morning and discovering "He's beeeen!!"
I saw myself playing football on the local field as a kid with my oldest bestest friends Daz and Kev..

I looked back on the many times my Sister and I had watched Forrest Gump together. It was our favourite film, especially when one of us was not feeling well.
There's a scene in that film, probably our favourite scene of all, where Forrest is sat by Jenny's bed as she lay dying. He was telling her about all the beautiful places he'd been and the adventures he'd seen. While she had been so far away living her own crazy life.
She just looks up at him and says "I wish I coulda been there with ya". His reply was beautiful, "You were.."
I think I was beginning to understand how you can be separated from your loved ones by miles, but still have them with you.
Always

I realised as I lay there that this is what really matters most in life.
And all of those cherished memories gave me a feeling of comfort, of home.

Many times in my life, before and since, I have thought I wouldn't live to see the morning.
And many times I've prayed to something, to

someone...

But during that time in Greece I truly believed I would never see those I loved again.

And I prayed for help, one more time...

My prayer was heard.

And almost miraculously, before too long, I found I began to feel well enough to leave the apartment. It was the first time I'd been outside in several days.

I eventually found a place to make a call to my Mum and Dad. I explained what had happened and, between us, we arranged my flights to come back home.

Thank God.

I didn't die in that room in the mountain in Greece. But I do believe I came to know what is truly important in life.

And once you know it, you can't ever un-know it..

So when people ask me why I'm not more interested in achieving 'Success'? Making a tonne of money, buying flash cars, eating in the poshest restaurants, or just proving anything to anyone? I tell them it's because in the end none of that stuff really matters much anyway...

I truly believe you've just gotta appreciate all those little things, the special - though sometimes ordinary - moments...

Especially when shared with family and friends.

Those moments of love and laughter.

Because that's what will bring you comfort when you look back someday.

You've gotta live a life you're gonna wanna look back on..

With a smile

'He Never Judged'

Puddy, or 'Pudsey' as I called him, was my little pal...
He was a black and white cat that we'd adopted
together with his brother, Bubbles, as kittens from a cat
rescue place close to where we lived.
I'm still not sure where those names came from?
Perhaps I'd named him after the 'Puddy Tat' I'd seen
in cartoons as a child. My Sister was always a Michael
Jackson fan, so maybe that's why she chose the name
Bubbles after his pet Chimp?
But straight away, even as a tiny kitten, Puddy and I
had a bond that was beyond special.

In the years that followed I would come to realise just
how important and special our little relationship really
was.
During those teenage years I was often in trouble and
sometimes it felt like the whole world was against me..
But Puddy would always be there.
He'd never judge and would fall asleep on my bed
every night purring his head off.
He taught me a whole lot about unconditional love that
little cat did.

So when I traveled to Israel at the age of 25 and knew
I'd be staying there a while I knew I'd miss my fluffy
mate and I had a feeling he'd miss me too...
But I also trusted that he would be in very safe hands.

After spending about 6 weeks traveling around the
country and being filmed for a documentary series
called 'Looking for Kicks' I'd decided to come back and

see everyone...

As usual my Dad picked me up from the airport. But as happy as I was to see him there were mixed emotions...

Bubbles had been really ill while I was away and had been put to sleep.

There was simply 'no choice'

But then I heard the rest, Puddy was also gravely ill...

So ill, in fact, that my parents had thought it may be 'his time' too.

But somehow he'd held on...

And I couldn't wait to see him.

I'd missed him so much. I gave him the biggest hug and even though he was so ill he slept on my bed that night just as he always had.

And during the night I had the most amazingly vivid dream.

I dreamt that I had been with Puddy at the vets when they'd told us there was really 'no choice'...

With tears in my eyes I'd cuddled him as he took his final breaths and went peacefully to sleep.

I can still remember the details so clearly.

The very next morning, Puddy took a serious turn for the worse.

I had never seen him like it before and it broke my heart.

I saw with my own eyes that we really had no choice. He was suffering so much...

I think he'd just waited to see me, to say goodbye.

I went with him and, just as I had seen in my dream the night before, the vet confirmed the worst.

Our decision was made and I hugged him exactly as I'd done in the dream...

Everything was the same
The details I had seen the night before were
being played out right before my eyes, even down to
the style of the metal table he fell asleep on.
It was something I'd never experienced in my
life before.

I brought Pudsey back home and carefully wrapped
him in one of my favourite jumpers.
We buried him, with a little prayer, at the bottom of the
garden.

I will never forget my special little mate, because he
brought so much joy to life...
He taught me a whole lot about love too...
He never turned his back on me once, no matter how
bad things ever got..
He stuck by me and he never judged.

It's the way I try to live my life to this day.

It was also then that I learned there is so much more
going on in our dream-world than we may ever know
or understand...
That was yet another gift he had given me

I will never forget that beautiful boy.

'Angels'

During the time I spent in Israel something quite
mysterious and beautiful had happened...
I'd visited all of the Holy sites, made some wonderful
friends and had quite a few fabulous adventures.
But on this one particular morning I'd woken
up especially early because I wanted to fulfil a simple
dream.
My dream was to walk along the walls around the old
city of Jerusalem...

I set off while it was still dark and there was barely
another soul about...and I made my way to a little place
I knew would lead me up onto the wall..
The view was stunning.
I just remember walking along that wall, as the sun
came up, feeling like I'd stepped back in history,
It all felt very special indeed.

Then, out of nowhere, all of a sudden the early
morning silence was broken...
"Heyyy, Hiii, how are you today" said a loud voice..
"Isn't it just so God-damn beautiful here"
It was an elderly, bizarrely attired American lady and
she was heading my way...
She asked if she could walk with me and, far too polite
to tell her I'd come for the solitude, I smiled and said
"Yeah, sure.."
We walked and talked about all sorts of things,
although mainly spiritual stuff as I remember.

Then she turned to me and said something that I really didn't expect...

"Would it be okay if I hold your hands, just for a moment. Only I'm receiving a message just for you"
It was odd, but so was she. Though I could tell she was very kind too..
So I said "Yeah, of course.."
She grabbed both of my hands and, facing me, she closed her eyes and went into some kind of a trance.
I still don't know if what she said next came from her or through her...
But, either way, I will never forget it...

"No matter where you go, or what you do, in this life there are angels by your side...
You will always be protected and you must never ever forget that"

It was a truly magical thing to hear, especially in those surroundings.
She told me that what had just happened had never happened to her before. Ever.
Then she pretty much apologised and went on her way.

There have been many times in my life since when I have reflected back upon what she said.. That morning, on the wall, above Jerusalem...
And if there are indeed angels somewhere close by, well, that would certainly explain a whole lot.

As the old man took his morning stroll along the beach he saw a figure up in the distance walking to and from the seashore...

There had been a storm the night before and thousands of starfish had been washed up on to the sand.

As he got closer he could see the figure was that of a young woman...

She was carefully picking up the starfish, one by one, before putting them back into the water.

The old man asked her exactly what she was doing?

"Oh, I'm just trying to help.. " she said

The old man looked around and could see there were starfish literally everywhere...

"I understand that..." he said to the girl "But there are so many. You really can't make any difference here I'm afraid.."

She just smiled, then calmly picked up another starfish, dusted him off and gently threw him back into the sea...

"Well.. " she said.. "I sure made a difference to that one!!"

'Kindness and the Kings Road'

It was totally surreal...

I had been coming here for years and had never seen the place quite like this before.

The King's Road, Chelsea, is usually so bustling and busy. But there was not another person in sight.

And everything was so very quiet... Barely a car, bus or taxi anywhere.

It was Christmas morning of the year 2000.

I was staying in a hotel just around the corner while volunteering for Crisis, an organisation that helps with homelessness in London.

I'd woken up early because I wanted to phone my family and wish them all a Happy Christmas.

But I will never forget that walk along the King's Road...

It was probably my favourite street in the whole wide world and I had so many different memories scattered along the length of it.

The very first time I'd walked along this road, many years before, I remember feeling as though I already knew it so well. It was somehow familiar. I already knew my way around. Perhaps from a past life, maybe during the swinging 60's...

I had often wandered up and down chatting to any homeless people there and trying to help them where I could.

And that evening I was hopefully gonna be helping them in a whole different kind of way...

Each Christmas, Crisis aim to get as many people off of the streets as possible. To give them shelter, food and a little entertainment. While also having all sorts of other advice and services available to help too. It's just a beautiful thing and I was so proud to be a part of it, even if only for a while.

When my shift came I was working alongside a Crisis veteran, Antonio, who had plenty of stories to tell that really did make me appreciate how worthwhile their work is.

It was one story though, above all the others, that stayed with me and made me realise just how important it is to care and to be kind.

Antonio told me how one day he'd been out and about in London, when he'd seen a homeless guy at the side of the road. Thinking to himself "There but for the grace of God go I" he offered the man a cup of tea and something to eat in a nearby cafe...

They sat and they chatted for a while and the homeless guy had shared with him his story.. It was a story of sadness, tragedy and loss...

Before he left, the homeless guy had asked the waitress for a napkin and a pen. Then he proceeded to scribble something down...

He thanked my friend Antonio for the meal and the chat and he passed him the napkin as he left.

On the napkin were written these words...

"Today, you've saved my life.

I had planned to end it all. My mind was made up. But you've shown me that people do care and that there is kindness in the world. You've renewed my faith and given me the strength to carry on.

Thank you from the bottom of my heart"

Hearing this story put tears in my eyes.

And it also reminded me of something I'd heard many years before.

There was a kid who was being bullied in school and things had become so bad that he had planned to take his own life.

He'd cleared out his locker of all his school books so that his parents didn't have to do that when he was gone. Then he headed home, with his mind made up to end it all. But on his way back home he stumbled and dropped some of the books he was carrying. Kneeling down to pick them up he noticed, out of nowhere, beside him, an older boy silently knelt down and began to help...

The older boy offered to help carry some of the books and they walked together and chatted until they reached the kids house. The older boy passed him back the books, smiled, and said goodbye.

I remember the kid, who was now a man, had told the story of how this simple act of kindness had saved his life.

Because he too had realised in that moment that not everyone was bad and that some people do care..

And it was enough to make him reconsider taking his own life.

The kid had actually gone on to be very successful in business and told this story years later while he was accepting an award. He'd dedicated the award to the older boy that walked him home that day...

The boy whose kindness saved his life.

Those two stories left me in no doubt that kindness is the most important thing in this world.

That the simplest act of caring can save a person's life.

'Time After Time'

Frinton is such a beautiful place...
On the Essex Coast of England, about 10 minutes from
my house, it has the most pristine sandy beaches and
an air of perfect tranquillity.
It's somewhere I would always come to, whenever I
needed a little help..
It had been my refuge, my sanctuary, my safe
place, ever since my school days.
I remember how, as a teenager, back when I was
always in trouble, with something always going on and
something always going wrong, I would just walk out of
the school and wander down here.
It's where I always knew I would find my happiness,
my peace.
I knew that would never change and it never has...

But this one particular night was a little special.

I had driven down to Frinton Sea-front at the end of
an extremely crappy day, during an especially hectic
period of my life.
I had a job, but I hated it. I had a tonne of debt. Plus I
almost always had some kind of woman trouble..
All in all, as I remember, I was just in a pretty bad way.

Looking back I think I was totally lost in my own life.

I parked up, got out of the car and, with tears in my
eyes, walked out across the green towards the edge
overlooking the sea...

Sensing no-one else was around, and with my mind in all sorts of turmoil, I was inspired to do something I'd never done before...

I shouted out to God...

Years before a friend had told me that, during a very difficult time in his own life, when his daughter was really ill, he'd asked God for some help. Some proof. Something. Anything, to let him know there was indeed a Higher Power.

A short while after doing this his daughter's condition had settled and almost miraculously she was well again very soon.

So with this at the back of my mind I remember looking up and just asking, pleading...

"God, where the fuck are ya??

Please.. I really need you now.. I really need to know..

I need to know you exist. Show me a sign. Please...

Anything. Something I will know for sure...

I wanna know you.

It's just us, here, now. Please show me"

There was nobody else around, it was dark, and here I was with tears in my eyes desperate to know for sure that something I'd sensed or felt my whole life actually exists.

Hoping someone, something, could hear me and help me.

I needed to know there was a higher power at work in our lives. At all times.

But I waited for my answer...

And I waited.. and I waited...

Looking back, I think perhaps I was hoping for a few shooting stars, maybe some fireworks, or something

else like that..
But after scouring the skies, and waiting for what
seemed like forever (but was probably no more than a
few minutes!) there was still nothing.
I felt so dejected, so utterly disappointed.
And with those tears still in my eyes I headed back to
the car...
I sat there for a while in the dark. Feeling pretty shit.
But more than anything.. Feeling totally alone...
Then, preparing for the drive home, I turned on the
radio...

It was in that exact moment that a song was playing
and I heard some words I will never forget..

"If you're lost you can look and you will find me..
Time After Time..
If you fall I will catch you, I'll be waiting..
Time After Time"

I remember a feeling that it's hard to describe. A feeling
that was coursing through my entire body...
I knew, I just knew...
It was my answer, my sign. Clearer than clear.

I turned the radio off almost straight away, but felt a
lightness that comes with having all of your worries
taken away...
Of knowing for sure that you are heard, known, loved
and understood...
And that something truly does have your back.

I've always said that God, or The Universe, works in
mysterious ways.
But I never expected some of the most important words
I would ever hear to come from Cyndi Lauper on

Frinton seafront...
And those words now mean more to me than anything.
They confirmed to me something that I had always
sensed anyway...
And, for that, I will be eternally grateful.

Many years ago in India a famous Guru was giving a talk to hundreds, perhaps thousands, of people.
The crowd was full of folks from all walks of life.
There were other Holy Men, Presidents, Film-stars, Musicians and many, many others...
When this man spoke it came from the soul. His voice was almost hypnotic and those present would literally become entranced by his words.

Once he'd finished speaking he asked if there were any questions? But it was unsurprising that there was only silence...
Everyone there was still absorbing what they'd just heard and seemed more than happy that every question had already been well and truly answered
Until eventually one man stood up...
He was a Western guy in a business suit, and half-laughing he said to the Guru, "Alright then, if you know everything, what's the meaning of life?"
The man was clearly trying to embarrass the Guru and to belittle him, but the Guru smiled and gently replied, "I'll answer your question, but first let me tell you something about yourself..."

Now this guy was the one that everyone was looking at and he became visibly uncomfortable.

The Guru continued.. "You have never been in love, have you?? he asked "Real, deep, true Love??"
"No", replied the man. Now slightly embarrassed himself, "No, that's true. I haven't.."
"Because..." said the Guru, "...any person who asks the question that you asked me about the 'Meaning of Life' is really only telling you something about themselves..

They have missed out on, or not experienced... true Love.

A person who knows real Love, from their own direct, personal experience, would never even ask that question, 'What is the Meaning of Life', because they would already know the answer"

The man smiled, thanked the Guru and sat back down... Understanding that Love is always the answer.

'Broken Valentine'

"This'll be romantical" I thought to myself as I queued up in the chocolate shop with a very clear vision of what I wanted...

It was the day before Valentine's Day.

There was a girl I knew in a local pub and she just had something about her. A beautiful kindness.

She was like an angel.

But I also knew she was unhappy and had a boyfriend that didn't treat her well...

So when it was my turn to order I asked if they could please write "For An Angel" on a big heart made all of chocolate.

The lady serving said it would be an absolute pleasure and when it was finally done she showed it to me and I was overjoyed.

It was just perfect. Far better than I'd ever imagined.

All I wanted to do was make this angel smile and I knew it would.

I'd had to drive a fair distance to find a place that I hoped could make such things. So after walking around town holding this beautifully boxed delicate chocolate message as if it were the most precious thing in the world, I carefully sat it down beside me on the passenger seat of the car... and then I set off home.

I'd done this journey a thousand times before and I still don't quite know what happened on this particular day... Perhaps I was going a little too fast, perhaps my music was a little too loud, maybe I wasn't paying enough attention, perhaps the road was just extra slippery?

All I know for sure is that I failed to make it around a bend and before I knew what was happening the car was flying off the road and through a field...

After that everything began to feel like slow motion.

The car started to roll... It rolled and rolled and rolled... While I was inside being thrown around like I was in a washing machine.

I saw the car miraculously leap a ditch, before it rolled some more and eventually came to a standstill... On its roof in the middle of the field.

I climbed out thanking my lucky, lucky stars. Shaken, but alive...

Some people had stopped at the side of the road to see what was happening and, perhaps because I'd seen too many films, I just ran to get as far away from the car as I could before it went up in flames.

But then I remembered.. "The Valentine's gift"...

There was no time to get another one now so I quickly ran back to the car and climbed in to grab it..

Still thinking the car may explode at any moment.

My beautiful gift was, unsurprisingly, in a thousand different pieces...

The box was all smashed up and the chocolate destroyed.

Still, I gathered the pieces together, put them all in the crumpled box and then asked to borrow someone's phone..

My family came, as they always had, to rescue me.

I had a few bumps and bruises, but I was in one piece. Which is much more than could be said for my gift!

It was actually my Grandpa's car and I will never forget the fact that all he cared about was that I was okay...

"It's only a car" he said "We can replace that.. We can't replace you"

That was him all over. The most important things to my family were never material things.
And I was fine. Thank God.

But that Valentine's gift appeared to be totally destroyed and it was far too late to get anything else now.
So after a little chat with my Sister and a few other very wise women it was decided that I would give the crumbs of chocolate to the angel in the pub anyway. Even though, by now, the message was unreadable.

The next day came and I handed her the chocolate remains, with a brief story of what had happened...
It turned out that her boyfriend had forgotten Valentine's altogether.
So when she told me it was the most romantical thing anyone had ever done for her, it kinda made it all worthwhile..
The smile on her face said everything
I'd made a little angel very happy...

Though I can't help but believe my own angels had been very busy indeed the day before.

'That Damn 27 Club'

I'd always had this strange feeling that I would die at 27
and become a member of that famous club..
Along with Jim Morrison, Brian Jones, Jimi Hendrix et
al...
But by the grace of God that never happened.
At least, not in quite the same way it did for them...
Something else happened instead...

First of all when I was a teenager, as I've said before,
I had been completely out of control. Off the rails.
Stupid.
I used to think it was so clever, so cool, to take as many
drugs as possible, to get as drunk as possible, to be as
crazy as possible.
And that almost back-fired a good few times!!
Most people in those days never thought I would reach
21, let alone 27.. And I continued with that lifestyle for
a good many years...
Psychologists would probably say I was trying to
fill some kind of void. Self-medicating, or whatever.
Perhaps due to the 'Primal Wound' of being adopted as
a baby?
Or maybe it was my Nanna dying when I was 11 and all
the confusion that came along with that??
Perhaps it was just finding I was in a life that was not
true to myself and trying in any which way I could to
escape...
But still, whatever the reason, I caused a lot of people
a lot of heartache and worry and for that I am deeply
sorry.
I know is that on some level I only wanted to feel

better in any way I possibly could.
Just to be accepted and to accept myself.
I guess I was looking for love...
But in all the wrong places.

Thankfully I slowly gave up all that utter recklessness
and gradually became more and more interested in
spirituality.
To me, that word spiritual really just means being
yourself, being natural. No more, no less.
Which is kinda cool when you understand that we're
not human beings having a spiritual experience. But
instead spiritual beings having a human experience..
We are in this world, but not of it.

For many years during my 20's I would go off on
strange travels all alone...
I would study every spiritual/sacred book going, I
would meditate often and meet with some of the
famous so-called guru's of the time.
It was a fun time, an interesting time and a very
healing time too.
One of the loveliest things I used to do, and still do now,
was go for those long walks by myself in nature.
That was my true meditation.
And it still is to this day.

My beloved Frinton is where I'd usually go for the most
blissful walks. I would either start there, finish there,
or just pass through there. But Frinton was always that
special place...
So it's kinda fitting that what happened on
1st September 2002.. happened there..
I still remember that date because, in a sense, it was the
day I died...
And I was 27 years old at the time.

Of course, I didn't die in the same way Jim, or Jimi.. or
more recently Amy Winehouse had.. but I died in a way
that all the spiritual paths talk about at some point...
I just had this deep and profound realisation of who I
was and my place in the Universe..
Which meant everything that wasn't really me died.

After walking for hours one evening I had found myself
heading back towards Frinton along the promenade,
totally alone, and by now it was almost dark...
For some reason that I will never really know
or understand I had this slightly uneasy feeling.
Something strange, that I had never felt before...
I'd recently heard a little mantra that I loved and I
slowly began to repeat it to myself;

"I am the love behind the fear. I am love behind the
fear"

Over and over, again and again. The uneasiness soon
subsided and I continued on...
It was shortly after that when something so damn
beautiful happened that it was to change my life
forever.

Even though it's almost impossible to put into words.
I'll try...

It was as though everything that wasn't really real just
disappeared.
As if everything dissolved that was not truly who I am.
It was like I was waking up for the very first time.
And as if Michelangelo's 'angel within' was
finally flying free.

I think the person we come to believe we are in day to day
life is really just a mind-made thing. An ego, if you will...

That aspect of ourselves is more of a mask, a defence, a shell...
Whereas the real truth of who we are, behind that mask, is far too beautiful even for words.
In my life I had always needed a defence, a mask, a shell, more than most...
But for just a few moments, perhaps because no-one was around, that all just simply disappeared...
And there was nothing left but a feeling of pure Love...
I will never forget it.

I don't mean the kind of love between a man and a woman, or a parent and a child.. just Love.. as a state of being.. an experience...
Just a feeling of total Oneness...
Which is extremely difficult to describe in words.
But it's what I'd been searching for my whole life. It was a love, a Oneness that I'd read so much about.
But now I was there.

And it was a feeling of absolute worthiness.
Completely timeless.
Boundless.

I stood there naked (with clothes on!) underneath the stars with tears of true joy rolling down my cheeks.
I looked up and around, at the vastness of All-That-Is, and all I could say was "Thank You"..
I understood everything, just for a while, with absolute clarity.
Every question I'd ever had was answered. Everything I had ever been searching for, I'd found.
On Frinton beach that September evening.

I'd often heard people say that you don't need to find yourself or learn anything, instead you just have to unlearn and remember what you've forgotten.

I knew right then and there just how true those words really were.

In that moment, for those moments, on Frinton seafront I was truly at Home..
I had returned to a place I somehow already knew, a state of perfect innocence.
Both timeless and deathless.
It's what I'd been searching for my entire life.
I don't really like to use the word God, as people have some strange ideas about what it means. But, ever since that day, I feel I understand it as an experience.
If I was a drop and God the ocean, the drop had become the ocean...
If only for a while..

Since that day I have never had the same drive to acquire material things or achieve things in the world.
I suppose I had been like everyone else and chasing the things I thought would fulfil me...
But here I was feeling the most profound bliss and true happiness without all those things I once thought I needed to feel like that.
So, right there and then, all that chasing of external 'stuff 'disappeared and never came back.
As cliched as it may sound, I just realised that it's all so true.. We are what we are seeking...
And who we are is enough...
Always.

It was the happiest I had ever been and the freeist too.
The most secure and the most 'In Love'..
There was a feeling of boundlessness that I'd never experienced before and haven't since..
A total freedom.

When something like that happens, and you feel like

that, with nothing and no-one to cause it... it changes everything...
I've often tried to put into words what happened that night, but it's almost impossible...
I guess there are some things that no words can come close to.
But it was then that I realised there's nothing we need that we don't already have...

It was a moment I touched the eternal.

I died, before I die... and so my fear of death disappeared forever.
But it was also a time I fell back in love with life
And it all happened at 27 years old...

So I kinda joined that club anyway.

'The Day I Met Her'

I stood there, by the Peter Pan statue, in Kensington Gardens holding the biggest bouquet of flowers I'd ever seen in my life and waiting...
I'd arrived early, probably to give myself some time to prepare...
But also to be sure she wasn't left waiting..

This area had always been very special to me.
I'd once walked through Hyde Park many, many years before when this extraordinary feeling came over me...
I just knew then that it would be a very special place in my life. That someday important events would unfold here...
It was as though my soul could already see it.

Now here I was on a cold beautiful November morning standing by the water waiting for the woman who had given birth to me 30 years earlier.

I had a very rough idea of what she looked like from the handful of pictures I'd seen...
And I had written her a letter a week or so before.
But as each person came around the corner I prepared myself as best as I could, without a clue how I would feel or what I would say...

And then I saw her.

As she got closer I just knew, she smiled and said something that I will never forget...

"Allo' Son, it's been a lonnnggg time.."

It was all so much easier than I'd ever imagined.
We hugged for a while and then decided to go for a walk around the park...
We just chatted about everything in life.
I wanted her to know, above and beyond anything, that I'd had a good life, a happy life, and that she'd done the right thing all those years ago.

She turned to me and asked if there was anything at all I wanted to know? What a question eh..
But in truth, my mind went blank and I couldn't think of anything.
I'd never really had many questions anyway...
Until, out of nowhere, "Yeah, is there any Irish in me" just kinda popped out..
I'd always loved Ireland and Irish things and never quite known why, so I was just interested...
She told me there was.

She said she'd been so nervous about us meeting, praying that everything would be okay..
Then she gave me a little something that had been given to her, by a priest, on the very day that I was born. He told her that someday she could give it to me...
She knew this day would come.
We both did.

Funny thing is, what she'd given me had some words written with it. They were all about trusting, and surrendering, to a higher power...
I'd had a very similar thing tattooed on my arm several years before...
So everything had just kinda come together perfectly...
As though it was all orchestrated by that same higher power.

It was a truly beautiful day.

'Jim'

On 28th September 2010... Something happened that brought new meaning and reason into my world and things would never be quite the same again.

Up until then, my whole existence had been based happily around not giving a fuck.

It was very much a 'Fuck It' lifestyle...

But in truth, I was kinda done. I'd had my fun and life had almost begun to bore me.

I'd spent soo many years soul searching. Found everything I'd ever searched for. Seen a bit of the world. And discovered the meaning of love..There was nothing left to do.

Or so I thought...

I had never really wanted my own kids, partly because I needed that freedom to be crazy, reckless...

I'd always thought "If it's just me, it doesn't matter. Whatever happens, happens. Live, die, not fussed.."

But at 12:15pm on 28/9/10 my little nephew James Paolo Allan came into the world.

And my whole world turned upside down forever. In the most beautiful ways imaginable.

I think perhaps the Universe understood that even though I didn't want children, I should get the chance to see what it was like to have one around...

Or maybe it was just looking after me (again!!) and it worked another miracle!

Either way, everything magically rearranged itself and

circumstances lined up in such a way that I would now be with this little bundle of wonderfulness... 'Jim'... every day.

He was a dream come true for sure.

But not just for me...

I remembered how many, many years before I had been out for a walk with my Sister, Mandy.

We were talking about everything; love, life, the past, the future and.. our dreams...

She was single at the time but told me how she dreamed of becoming a Mum someday.

She said that was all she ever wanted, just to be a Mum.

And even though she wasn't fussed whether she had a boy or a girl, I remember how she went on to dream..

"Can you imagine if I had a boy.. and got to call him Jim (after the singer Jim Morrison).. Ohhh how amazing would that be"

Well, her dream eventually came true down to the finest detail...

In the most wonderful way imaginable.

I loved my little Nephew from the first moment I saw him at just a few minutes old.

As time went by we developed a bond deeper and more special than anything I had ever thought possible...

I looked after him, and he looked after me.

One day it dawned on me and I realised I had fallen in love with life all over again.

I actually gave a fuck!! For the first time in a long time.

Soon I would prefer days in the park, to all those nights in the clubs/pubs...

My proudest happiest moments had become the joy of seeing him do new things, make new friends.. Helping him learn to read or to ride a bike... His very first day of school...

It was like a lovely light had been switched on, yet I hadn't even realised it was dark.

It was quite simply the best thing that ever happened to me.

To cut a long story short... Little Jim pretty much saved my life.

I don't know if he did that literally, but maybe.. Because that crazy existence was killing me slowly.

But more importantly he brought such meaning back to life.

I had searched for myself, for God, for Nirvana, for love in all sorts of places.. On the beaches, in the forests, through drink/drugs, around the world, and deep inside...

But this little man, more than anything else in the world, reminded me who I really was and why I was here...

He made me want to be a better person.

He reminded me how much life was really worth living...

And he brought my life back to life...

It was fun again!!!

To top it all off he is now growing up to be the most wonderful, awesome little guy I could ever have hoped or imagined.

I am soo very proud of him every day in every way.

I suppose I owe a big thank you to God, the Universe, Source Energy, or whatever, for bringing our lives together...

That divine power and intelligence that just knows what you need and when you need it...

I've always believed in that, always known it...

And the timing is always perfect

That much I know for sure

'A Pint A Day'

So there we were, just sat watching Spongebob
Squarepants The Movie when little Jim, who was now
3, asked for another bottle of milk...
I told him "You've only just had one mate!! Are you
sure??"

"I love it Uncle Siyo" he said "And it makes my Winkie
grow!!"

I was utterly speechless..But I got him his milk.
In fact I had a pint of it myself too.
Looking back I think that was the moment I swapped
pints of beer for pints of milk...

The benefits seemed just too good to be true

'A Little Deer Story'

Set in the Suffolk countryside, Alton Water is pretty much a great big lake surrounded by a nature reserve and it was another of my favourite places to visit.
It's just beautiful.
It would take about 3 hours to walk around and on a nice day it was quite literally the best meditation I knew.
I would often spend my days there soul-searching, meditating, making peace with the past and plans for the future.
But more than anything else just enjoying the moments, one by one...
On this one particular occasion I was about half way around the 7-8 mile circuit when I stopped for a break.
Looking around me I saw a sign I'd never ever seen before. It was pointing in a slightly different direction and said "Follow this route for a chance to see Deer"...
Well, this was news to me. I'd been here countless times and never knew there were deer about.
So as I continued on my walk I was looking everywhere. Over fences, across fields, in tiny forests... just hoping to spot a deer.
But there was nothing.
Around about this time I was very into the whole idea of 'Creating your life and destiny'.. Asking the Universe.. The law of attraction.. Manifesting and so on.. So I thought I'd put all this to the test.
With no-one else around I quietly asked the Universe, or God, to help me see a deer. and then I continued on my way...
Looking here, there and everywhere...
But still, nothing.

I just remember feeling so disappointed.

I was starting to think "What a load of rubbish!!! The Universe doesn't listen!!"

Even though deep down I knew that wasn't true...

Finally, in a moment of clarity, but exasperation, I remember looking up and saying "For fucks sake, there's no-one here. Just show me a goddamn deer!! I wanna know all this stuff is really real. Show me a deer. Pleeease!!!"

I was more than a little frustrated and upset..

But still, I saw nothing.

And after a while I just gave up. I thought to myself "Fuck it!!. I'm here, I'm just gonna enjoy it. Who cares about the damn deer.."

It was such a beautiful day and I wasn't gonna let this spoil it...

Then...

Moments later I turned around...

And there it was.

The most beautiful little Bambi like creature I ever did see.

A gorgeous little deer stood within a few feet of me.

Just looking up at me...

It was one of the most profound and beautiful experiences of my entire life.

I thanked God and did my best to apologise. Afterall, my faith in everything was restored..

But as I continued on my walk, and over the years since, I have understood so much more clearly what had really happened that day..

Life has taught me many times since that you can have anything you desire. If you can dream it, you can be it, do it, have it...

I know that for sure. Ask and it IS given.

But the secret is that once you've asked you've also got

to have a deep trust...
Enough faith to be able to just relax and let go.

You've gotta find a way to trust enough to just give up...
Almost not care if it happens or not...
And let the Universe do its work...

That's when it always happens.

A young man was sitting there on the dock, fishing, with a very contented look upon his face.

An older rich guy would often see him and wonder who he was and why he was always there?

One day the older guy approached the younger man and he asked him "Heyy, why don't you go study or get a job??"

The young man looked up, smiled, and asked "Why?"

The rich guy was puzzled.. "Well, because you could earn yourself some money"

The man again replied.. "Why??"

By now the older guy was getting annoyed, "Well, because you could do all sorts of stuff then, you could even buy yourself a nice boat one day"

The young man asked again.. "But why?"

"Well.." said the rich man.. "You could catch sooo many fish that way and you'd earn yourself a fortune!!!"

But the younger man replied "Why?"

The rich guy was furious.. "Because then you could do WHATEVER you wanted to!!" he screamed..

"I'm doing that now" came the reply...

'They Wonder, I Wander'

My working life (aka career) was pretty scattered and varied for years.

So many jobs, in so many places, but something was always amiss...

I did what I was most qualified to do. But too many times I had this feeling, like I was just selling my life by the hour.

I always knew there had to be more...

Nowadays, even if they never say it out loud, I know that many people must quietly wonder why I don't work harder 5/6/7 days a week?

They see me out for a walk in the sun, picking Jim up from school, or being tagged on social media in all sorts of weird and wonderful places and they ponder "Why isn't he at work?"

Well, I've never really cared what people think. Ever.

But, if I were to answer that question the simple truth is... Because I just don't need to be.

I'm not financially rich - by any stretch of anyone's imagination - and I've never had any real desire to be... Although I do feel rich in so many other ways.

Don't get me wrong, if I had kids I would do whatever had to be done - literally - to give them a good life.. But I don't have kids...

I just have those memories of sitting at a desk in a posh office many years ago looking at the clock and thinking "What the fuck am I doing??"

Until one day I just walked out and never went back.

So the life I have that looks very strange to many is actually the life I once dreamed of...

And these days I do what I enjoy, then I do what I have to do to get by and it's all good.

So do I wish I was back in the 'rat race', so unhappy that I was spending all my hard-earned money on drink and drugs just to fill the void? No.

Been there done that!

Do I wish I had more money so that I could buy a faster car, a better phone, a shinier watch.. to impress other people...

No.

Never been there, never done that!

I say this perhaps to inspire people to look at what they're doing and why...

I see folks everywhere trying to prove their worth, trying to justify their own existence through accomplishments.

And there's no need.

We are all born worthy, we'll all die worthy.

Worthiness is no issue at all.. It's a given.. I discovered that back on the beach at 27 years old..

You can't not be worthy. No matter who you are or what you've done...

Nothing can ever change that.

So why don't I just do what I love?

Well, I do. Every single day...

I write, I try to help others, and I play a role in bringing up one of the most wonderful little people ever.

And I have never been happier. Truly.

So to anyone that may look at me and feel sorry for me as they drive past on their way to somewhere they don't really wanna go...

I'm perfectly fine. Thank you.

Though if you are doing that for your kids I salute you and I respect it totally.

But just remember this - There is not one recorded instance of anyone on their death-bed wishing they'd worked longer hours...

So go live a life that you love, if you can...
And fuck what they say!!!

'She Came To Me'

It was about a week before my Grandpa died and I had just been in to say goodnight to him...

He knew his illness was terminal, but had never once complained or seemed afraid in any way.

I had been with him in the hospital when they gave him the news...

And he accepted it so gracefully.

His only wish was that he stay at home, in my parent's house, surrounded by everyone he loved.

We would all take it in turns to visit, sit with him, tell jokes, perhaps watch some football, or do a crossword.

But he had gradually declined and eventually was pretty much confined to his bed.

All my life he'd been my partner-in-crime, my bestest friend, my rock and my place to run to...

He had always been there for his family. But now it was him that needed us.

On this particular day, after I'd said goodnight, he called me back and he said something that I will never forget...

"She came to me. She came to see me, Son. Your Nanna. Iris. She came.. And.. She still loves me.."

Then he fell asleep with the most beautiful smile on his face.

My Nanna had died when I was 11. But they'd been married for almost 50 years. She was his soulmate...

I have an open mind about everything. But he knew what he had experienced...

And it brought him sooo much peace.

I can still remember the loveliest story I'd heard about a time when he and my Nan had only just got together. They'd had a silly argument about something and she'd stormed off telling him "I never want to see you again!!"
And she apparently meant it too.
Still, a few days later, my Grandpa was sitting there contentedly making a rug for her...
A friend walked over to him and gently said "What are you doing?? She's gone. I'm so sorry, but she has.."
Grandpa smiled, continued what he was doing and replied "Ahhh, but she'll be back"
And a few days later she was.
Love would always bring those two back together again.

On the day he died I was once again at his bedside.
My sister and I had been talking to him, reading to him and playing him his favourite music.
The Doctors and Nurses recommended this even though they couldn't work out how he was surviving so long,
By now he was in a coma and pretty much non responsive in any way.
I remember how we'd been playing him a song called 'Seven Tears' that I'd listened to at his house as a child.
As it played I'd reflected back on how I would run around the garden of the big London house we all lived in. I would run and run, as fast as I could. Always in the sunshine. Always happy.

We had so many wonderful memories between us.

A nurse had suggested that perhaps the reason he may be hanging on was that he needed to know it was okay to just let go??
So while everyone else was downstairs I decided to

have a quiet word with him.
Just us..
Like we'd done ever since I was a little kid.

Not many people know this, but this is what I said to him...
"It's okay Grandpa. You go where you've gotta go. We are all fine. You go see her. You go Home..
I'll come and see you soon"

Within 20 minutes he had taken my advice...
Peacefully and surrounded by everyone he loved...
He'd finally let go.
He'd gone home.

So do I miss him? Yep, every single day.. But do I know he is in a beautiful place and I will see him again? For sure.
And do I believe my Nan came to visit him just before he died? Yes, I do. I actually think he kinda had a foot in both worlds for quite a while...
I do know something for certain though.. Love is so much stronger than death..
I have always known that.
And I know it partly because I still love him dearly and I always will.

If this life has taught me one thing above all else it's that love is the only really real thing there is.
It's all that ever matters.
Truly, madly, deeply.

'Rainbows'

As the helicopter flew over Central Park I had the
sudden realisation that this was truly a dream come
true.

A few days before I had been walking through
that park, on my way to Strawberry Fields, as a
children's choir began to sing 'Let It Be'...
It was an incredible moment.
That had always been a favourite song of mine and
'Letting go', 'Letting it be' had been something of a
theme that had followed me throughout my life.
It was my greatest lesson to learn..

My Grandpa had died just a few months previously...
I'd come here to try and get myself together, make a
few special memories and stay with a friend who had a
place in the East Village.
This helicopter ride had always been a dream and my
Grandpa had known that.
He had left me some money which I knew he would've
been so happy to see I was spending on this.
As the helicopter flew over the Statue of Liberty I
closed my eyes and said a silent little 'Thank You, mate'
For everything.. and especially for making this all
possible.
Moments later we came in to land by the river...
And what happened next took my breath away.

There's probably a very simple explanation for it...
No doubt something to do with the sunshine and the

spray of the water.

But all I could see out of each window were rainbows all around us...

Everywhere I looked...

It was one of the most beautiful sights I had ever seen.

There was a big smile upon my face and it was almost as if my Grandpa was right there with me...

Perhaps, in a beautiful way, he was..

'Dreams Do Come True'

Hyde Park, London, had always been my little place of peace.

I guess it's my equivalent of Audrey Hepburn's 'Tiffany's'...

It's just full of beautiful and happy memories.

There's one particular spot in the park which overlooks the length of the Serpentine and, if I had to choose, I'd say that spot is probably my favourite...

Many years ago I had been to some kind of spiritual talk somewhere in London and was passing through the park by this favourite spot...

I'm still not sure why, but I looked out over the water and asked the Universe that the next time I stood here my whole life would have been "transformed by the power of love"

I still don't know what made me ask. But I guess I was ready to fall in love, perhaps meet that someone special, or just understand love itself a little deeper.

It was only for fun and so I went off and pretty much forgot all about ever asking. Although, strangely enough, I didn't pass by that exact spot for a few years after that...

Then one day I happened to be out in London with my sister Mandy and Nephew Jim and we decided to cut through the park. Maybe pop to the playground for a while...

Without even realising we just so happened to walk past the exact spot that I had made the wish years earlier and I suddenly remembered...

Then I looked down at little Jim (who was not even born when I'd stood there last) and I suddenly realised...

My prayer had been answered.

My life had been turned around completely...

And by the power of love.

I even had the little guy with me who was responsible!!

Life has taught me time and time again that you can be/do/have anything at all, as long as you believe it's possible.

You just have to let go a bit, give up caring so much, perhaps even forget you've asked...

One thing I do know for sure is that this Universe works in mysterious and such very clever ways.

So just trust...

And then watch all those dreams come true.

Much more recently I had been in to tuck Jim into bed and he caught me by surprise when he asked me to tell him a story...

It was getting late, but I really couldn't say no...

The trouble was I couldn't think of a good story. My mind just went blank. So I told him this story above about Hyde Park, as it involved him and I'd only recently written it.

He listened until the end and then smiled the biggest smile...

Then he asked "Do you want to hear my story, Uncle??"

I said "Yes, please.. I'd love to mate"

He looked at me and then he began... "Well, it was before I was even born and I remember I was talking to God...

I asked him to please give me the happiest family who would love me forever...

My dream came true too"

It was the most beautiful thing I'd ever heard.

A young couple had recently become parents to their second child, a little girl...

They already had a Son of 5 years old.

The boy soon began to ask if he could spend some time alone with his new baby Sister?

But the parents were concerned...

They'd heard all sorts of stories about jealousy and sibling rivalry.

However, the little guy was very persistent and eventually they gave in. They let the little boy into the room where his baby Sister was laying in her cot...

Then they left them both alone. Making sure to leave the door slightly ajar so that they could see and hear everything that was happening.

The little boy walked over to the cot and stood there for a while just looking in...

And this is what they heard him say next...

"Please, please try and remember.. What does God look like..

Please tell me..

Because I'm starting to forget"

'Monster Wave'

From the moment we arrived in Portugal we absolutely loved it.

We'd come to stay in a beautiful villa for a short break in the Algarve. Myself, my Mum, my Dad, Mandy and, of course, little Jim

Most of our time was spent lounging around the villa by day, while at night my Sister and I would venture into town to the bars and clubs. We loved it.

On this one particular day we'd decided to walk down to the local beach, Praia de São Rafael.

It was absolutely stunning.

My Mum and Sister wanted to catch some sun, while my Dad was taking some pictures of the cliffs surrounding the beach.

I played in the sand with Jim.

A few days before I had promised to take him into 'The Ocean' for the very first time in his life...

And I should've known he would never ever forget... "Can we go in Uncle? Please, please. I wanna go swimming.."

Well, I had promised and I don't break a promise so I said okay and in we went..

Jim had never been further than the shallow end of a swimming pool.

He couldn't swim a stroke and had only ever paddled in the sea, but we were hoping that during this trip he would learn to swim.

For now though, I was carrying him in my arms and he was loving every second of it.

Even though everything around us looked so beautiful I had noticed earlier that the sea was actually pretty rough...

So I knew we wouldn't venture in too far.

I decided what I would do is just go deep enough that he felt like he was swimming, even though I would actually still be holding him...

He loved it. He was smiling, laughing and just generally having the time of his life...

Until...

All of a sudden there was a steep drop and my feet could barely touch the ocean floor!

It was frightening...

But not as frightening as what happened next...

The biggest wave I had ever seen was heading straight for us and it was truly one of the most terrifying experiences of my entire life..

I managed to keep Jim above the water but the force of the wave, along with the current, had somehow pulled us out even further.

My feet could no longer touch the floor, I had Jim in my arms and now we were being pummeled by wave after wave after wave..

I was struggling to breathe and all I knew was that I had to somehow keep Jim's head above the water..

And somehow I managed to do just that.

Thank God.

Eventually the force of the waves had actually thrown us both back again, far enough that I could touch the sea-floor for the first time in what seemed like forever...

But, I was so tired I fell over and was once again struggling to keep little Jim above the water.

I quickly looked around for help and all I could see was my Dad, who was filming the whole thing and my

Sister and Mum smiling and waving from a distance..
I felt totally and utterly drained, while everyone around thought we were having the best time of our lives!
The only thing I know for sure is that Jim stayed above that water throughout the whole thing..
Although I've no real idea how.

Eventually I was able to drag us both far enough up the beach, out of reach of the waves, where we could finally get our breath back..
But I'll never forget it...
Neither will Jim...
He still talks about the 'Monster Wave' to this day.

While the whole experience was more than a little traumatic it did also teach me something very beautiful and profound...
I now totally understand when parents say they would die for their children in a heartbeat.
It's such a powerful thing. An instinct.
Even while I was under that water, I knew he'd be okay and he did too. The little guy always knew that I would never let him down (or drown!!). In fact, a few minutes later he wanted to go straight back in the water again!!!
Although I was far too exhausted!!

I have said many times before how truly magical it is when a little child puts their hand into yours as you both cross the road..
Because they are basically trusting you with their life.
And I think having that kind of trust with any other human being is just about the best thing ever.

Jim can now swim like a fish and could probably save me if I was drowning...
But he knows, without a doubt, that I would be there

for him and even die for him if I had to.

We have such a special bond and understanding.
And I know we'll be there for each other
Always

During a certain period many years ago there was a civil war ravaging a distant land...

And there was this one particular General who had the most fearsome, violent reputation...

As his army was rampaging through the country they would usually find that towns and villages had all been deserted by the time they arrived. People were fleeing for their lives.

So when they arrived at another village only to find it deserted, they were not in the least bit surprised...

But, while searching, they were amazed to discover a lone Monk just sat on a mat meditating...

The soldiers immediately alerted the General.

He was enraged. He enjoyed the fact that everyone was running and that everyone was scared of him.

He demanded to see the Monk.

He looked down at the peaceful Monk and he bellowed "What are you still doing here? Don't you know who I am?"

The Monk just smiled and said "No Sir, I do not"

This infuriated the General even further and he drew his sword...

"Well, I am the one you may have heard about. The one who can cut off your head without batting an eye"

The Monk smiled again...

He looked up at the General and said to him "Do you know who I am, Sir?"

The General was fuming and he shouted "No, who are you?!!"

"Well, I am the one who can have his head cut off without batting an eye" replied the Monk...

The General was speechless...

He bowed to the Monk and left him alone in peace

'The Phone Rang'

My family had all flown off to Portugal for another holiday in the place they'd fallen in love with...
They were all so excited to be going back, especially little Jim.
My plan was to pop out and join them for a week or so while they were there,
But as I waited patiently for the phone call to say they'd arrived safely and all was well it never came... and I knew something wasn't quite right.

Eventually though a call did come and it was from my Sister...
She was utterly distraught and it was also a bad line.
But, from what I could make out, she was saying "Now, try not to worry... But Dad's been rushed off in an ambulance! He's fallen down some stairs at the airport. He looked real bad.."
Then, just like that, she was gone and my mind started racing...
What had happened?? Why had he fallen?? Had he had a stroke?? Had he had a heart attack?? Was he even alive??
I immediately looked for flights but couldn't find anything until at least the following day. Although the last thing my Sister had said was that she would phone back that evening and not to do anything until then...
So I did what I've always done at a time like that. I went for a walk...

I walked wayyyy out into the middle of nowhere, with my head spinning and tears in my eyes...

Then I did something else I've always done at a time
like that...
I said a quiet prayer..
I just asked that everything would somehow be okay
and that my Dad would be alive and I could get there to
help...
The funny thing is, in that moment I felt such
a beautiful sense of peace...

When I got back home I made something to eat and
just sat there. Waiting. Looking out of the window. Not
knowing what on earth to do next...
And that's when the phone rang....

It was my Dad.

He was calling from the hospital.
He was totally shaken up and with a badly broken
ankle, but he was alive.... And there was no stroke, no
heart attack..
My prayers had been answered.
Once again.

Within a few days I was at his bedside in the
Portuguese hospital, giving him a hug, telling him I
loved him and sneaking him in some 'proper food'.
But I will never forget those moments when I felt truly
powerless and afraid...

There have been many times in my life that I've found
myself with literally nowhere to turn and I've always
done the same thing.. Looked up.
To God, The Universe, or any kind of a higher power...
Every single time I've ever asked for help, it's been
given...
Again and again and again...

So I guess the moral of the story is never be afraid to ask for a little divine assistance. It's there...

It's always there.

But also to remember that everything in this life can change in the blink of an eye.

I'd waved everyone off in the early hours that morning not even contemplating that something like that might happen.

In the rush I'd forgotten to tell everyone how much I loved them...

And we should always tell those we love how much we love them...

Life's far too short and uncertain to leave such important words unsaid.

'Lawnmower vs. Wifi'

The sun was shining the birds were singing and it seemed like the perfect day to do my least favourite job in the world... Mow the lawn.

But with a smile on my face and a spring in my step I set to work. Determined to make the best of it.

I'd almost finished both the back and the front and was actually quite impressed with my own handiwork. It wasn't quite Centre Court at Wimbledon, but close..

Still I was happily 'In the zone', whistling, singing, zoned-out perhaps, daydreaming when I heard the biggest bang and a strange jolt went through my body...

I knew straight away what I'd done...

I'd mowed right through the electric cable.

I actually thought this kind of thing was fatal!

But thankfully my Dad had fitted some kind of a trip switch which meant all that happened was the electricity in the house cut out.

"Thank you Dad. Thank you God. Thank you my Guardian Angel"

I sat down next to what was left of the lawnmower and just thanked my lucky stars.

In that exact moment a car pulled up with my Sister and little Jim inside...

And I hugged them both as though I'd just been pardoned from death row. Jim looked up at me, puzzled, and asked "Are you okay, Uncle.."

I told him what had happened and that his beloved Uncle was lucky to be alive...
His face dropped and I thought he was about to cry...

And that's when he said it...

"So does that mean we've got no Wifi??!!"

There were two Monks, an older one and a younger one, out for a walk one afternoon...

Their route had taken them to the bank of a fast flowing river.

As they approached the edge they could see further along there was a young woman looking very distressed...

So they walked over to her and asked her what was wrong?

She explained that she couldn't swim, but needed to get across and was so scared...

The older Monk immediately offered to carry her across on his shoulders.

She was overjoyed.

When they eventually reached the other side he gently put her back down again.

She thanked them and went on her way, as they went on theirs...

But there was a strange silence between the Monks as they continued on their journey.

Eventually the younger Monk could contain himself no longer... and he blurted out...

"What on earth were you thinking? You know we are forbidden from touching a woman...

And you put her on your shoulders like it was nothing!!"

The older, wiser, Monk smiled..

"Ahhh yess, indeed I did. I saw she was in need and I wanted to help her...

But I put her down way back there...

You, my friend, are still carrying her"

'42 Years Old'

My early evening stroll had taken me right past the entrance to a beautiful church very near to where I live.

It's such a picturesque little place, in the middle of fields, with a 'Bluebell Wood' right next door to it...

I'd always joked that if ever I got married, it would be here.

Just as I passed by, an old man was getting out of a car carrying a bunch of flowers and what appeared to be a bottle of vodka...

It was an unusual thing to see, to say the least.

As I got even closer I noticed he'd been crying and it looked like he was about to say something to me...

"My Son's been buried here 18 years today.." he said "He would have been 60 years old now.."

I was totally lost for words and told him how deeply sorry I was.

I told him I'd remember him and his Son whenever I walked past that spot again.

We spoke for a short while, before I headed on my way...

But as I walked I did a quick calculation and realised his Son must have died at 42...

The exact same age as I was.

So many things went through my mind. It could have all been so very different...

I thought of all those times I 'nearly didn't make it' and how fortunate I was to be here, healthy, and able to go

for a beautiful stroll like this...
I reflected on everything that had happened in my life.

If this life experience has taught me anything it's that
you really never know when your time is up...
That it's just so important to try and enjoy each and
every moment...
To be as happy as you can be and try and make life
better, easier and happier for others too.
Also to let go of, or not carry, all of the baggage and
negativity that so many feel they have to drag around
with them...
I think that real enlightenment is just about lightening
up a little.
Laughing, having fun, and not taking everything so
seriously...
And to love one another...
There's really no greater way to live than that.

There was a pond nearby and I stood and stared for a
while at the evening sunshine reflecting on the water.
This had been my favourite sight all my life. I always
imagined it's what Heaven must feel like.
No matter where I was in the world, this sight had
always felt like Home.

Someone once said .. "What will survive of us, is love..'
And that dear little old man reminded me, once again,
how true that really is..

'Heaven Is Here. Now'

It was one of the most beautiful days of the year so far and I'd decided to take myself off for a little bit of nature therapy.

It turned into a day of walking and meditation in some of the most sublime surroundings imaginable.

The sun was shining, the flowers were in bloom, there was blossom on the trees, butterflies everywhere and the birds were singing...

Life was just about as good as it gets.

I even sat for an hour on a bench in the gardens of the Crematorium near to where I live, which was like a little Garden of Eden that time of year...

This was the place where the funerals of both my Nanna and Grandpa had taken place.

As evening drew closer I decided I'd go for the longest stroll ever...

Through the fields, past the forests and off into places that even I had never been before.

It soon became one of the most peaceful, serene times of my entire life.

As I was heading back home I was walking towards the setting sun, surrounded by a stunning, almost mystical, light mist, with a bright shiny full-moon directly behind me...

Everything was in such perfect alignment.

It was like being in Nirvana...

So much so, that I decided to sit down for a moment under a tree...

As I sat there for a while I imagined how Buddha must've felt sitting underneath his tree all those centuries ago...

After years of searching and seeking he'd pretty much given up and, as is often the way, that was the moment when the Universe gave him more than he could ever have imagined..

I once heard a story that after this happened he spent days, maybe weeks, just laughing...

People would come up to him and ask "Heyy, what's up with you?"

And he would explain to them that he'd spent years searching for something that he'd had all along...

That 'enlightenment' is just our own true nature...

He found the whole thing so funny...

I always loved that.

I've often said to people that someday you will find yourself in a moment that's perfect in all ways and in that moment you can look back on your life and see how everything had to happen exactly as it did...

This really was one of those moments.

But then all of a sudden something very, very unexpected happened...

I started singing...

Not out loud, just under my breath.

Still, those who know me well know that singing is not something I should ever do...

But, it was happening anyway.

And the funniest thing of all was that I knew the words I was singing, but had no idea of the song...

Lyrics were just coming out of nowhere..

"When I feel alone, I reach for you..

And you bring me home...

"In this world we're just beginning,
To understand the miracle of living.."

I was baffled, because I knew it... I just didn't know
where from...
It was the strangest, craziest thing ever!

Then, after a little while, it all came flooding back... It
was Belinda Carlisle's 'Heaven Is A Place On Earth'
And just realising that made me smile the biggest
smile...
I'd not even heard the song in years, yet here I was
singing it, without knowing, in the middle of a place
that could only be described as Heavenly...
It was one of the most beautiful experiences of my
entire life.

I walked the rest of the way home kinda 'blissed-out'...

And I thought about when Belinda first sang that song
back in the 80's...
I was about 12 years old.
My Nanna had just died and I was just a kid. Not
knowing what lay ahead of me. All of the craziness,
beauty and adventure...
I remember hearing Belinda singing those words and I
kinda fell in love with her...
I believed every word she was saying..

I looked back on the future I'd been dreaming of then
and I smiled again,
Life had been so good to me. In all its ups and downs I
could only see beauty..

And when those words, those lyrics, come to you direct
from your own soul, from the Universe...

Well, the song takes on a whole new and very special meaning...

I knew that Heaven really is a place on earth.

'All Is Right With The World'

There we were, sat on the edge of the duck-pond chatting about life.

Jim and I would often do this together...

We loved it and it gave his Mum a chance to get dinner ready or do a few of the things she had to do.

We would talk about everything; love, girls, school, ducks, anything...

I think we just enjoyed sitting there side by side.

On this particular day Jim was telling me about school...

He told me that each of his friends had been talking about what their Dad's do for work., "My Dad's a Fireman" said one.. "My Dad's an Accountant" said another....

Jim had told them "Well, my Uncle has two jobs.."

I smiled, but was kinda baffled...

"Oh really, and what are they??" I asked him

"To give me fun and keep me safe" he replied

It put tears in my eyes...

That is exactly what I had promised Mandy I would do before he was even born.

I gave him the biggest hug and we set off home.

He told me they'd asked him in school what he wanted to be when he grew up and he'd told them "I don't want to grow up. I want to be just like my Uncle.."

That made me laugh.

I guess I was something of a Peter Pan afterall...

But I asked him, in all seriousness "What do you wanna be when you grow up, little buddy??"
His reply was instant "Happy. Like I am now"

I looked down at him and then up at the sky as the sun was about to set...
In that exact moment all was perfectly right with the world...

We were both truly happy
We were home

About the Author

Simon Heighway has enjoyed writing from a very early age and has had a lifelong interest in spirituality. Born in London and now living in Essex, England, Simon's very early life experience set him off on a journey of the soul, a journey home. This journey has taken him to many places and lead him to try many different things. Ultimately the search lead him back to his true self. Many of his reflections on this journey have already been enjoyed by countless readers across the world.

Printed in Great Britain
by Amazon